The Wisdom Seed

Revealing the Mystery of the
Thousand-Dollar Seed

The Wisdom Seed

Revealing the Mystery of the
Thousand-Dollar Seed

J. Anthony Gilbert

ISBN 979-8-9862151-5-0

Visit: www.anotherlevel.church
pastorj@anotherlevel.church

Published by FUSION Publishing Group, Butler, PA 16002

Dedication

To the men and women of God who paved the way in the midst of persecution to teach us the principles of seed faith giving. Thank you for your faith and example.
I salute you.

Table of Contents

Introduction:

Something Happens at the Thousand-Dollar Level

PART 1: Understanding the Wisdom Seed

PART 2: Activating the Wisdom Seed

Final Thoughts

Introduction

Something Happens at the Thousand-Dollar Level

The message of seedtime and harvest is not a thing of the past. It is more alive now than it has ever been. The Bible says in Genesis 8:22, "As long as the earth remains, seedtime and harvest, cold and heat, winter and summer, day and night shall not cease." This means that as long as you see cold, heat, winter, summer, and the sun rises and sets, you can count on the fact that you will reap what you sow.

Have people abused it? Yes! Have people misunderstood it? Yes! As a result, has the devil exploited this? Yes! But does this make it wrong or make it null and void? No! Let me start from the top. This revelation you are about to read will catapult your thinking to a new level. I am so convinced of seedtime and harvest that even if it was not in the Bible, I would still follow it because it works.

How many of you have heard this statement before: "There is something that happens at the Thousand-Dollar Level"? If you are like me, you have heard it hundreds of times. One day it hit me. It was like God said to me, "Jay, do you want to know what happens?" So, with my inquisitive mind, I said, "Yes, Lord!"

Since I was a little boy, I have always been a giver. I do not think there has been a dollar I have received that I did not tithe off. From the time I was very young, I have seen that when you give, God blesses you. I have given sacrificially from the time I was very young and have seen God bless me. However, it was not until I was much older that I gave a thousand dollars for the first time. I was so excited the first time I ever did it. It was not my parents' money or something someone gave me. I earned this money, and God put it on my heart to sow.

Something happened way back then that blessed me. However, I did not know what that "something" was that happened at the Thousand-Dollar level, but every time I did it, "something" always happened.

I am so excited that you have picked up this book. I believe that God is going to open your eyes, and you are about to see wondrous things in His word.

I have always believed in the power of sowing and the message of seed time and harvest. Many people scoff at the message, but I truly believe in its power and that God gave it to us to bless us.

Think about it for a moment; the message of the seed has always been in the bible. But its revelations over the last 75-80 years have been outstanding. Why did God reserve it for now? Why are we the generation that has been entrusted with it? I believe it is because a transfer of wealth has been prophesied, and God wants to know who He can give through, not just who He can give to. You are going to have to ask yourself in this season, can God trust me? Do I want to be a person that God gives through in this season?

Now, I do not believe that you can sow your way out of everything. But I do believe it is a start, and it can begin the process. I believe stewardship is also important. You can sow, and God can begin to bless you, but you can lose it if you do not understand how to steward the harvest. It is the same thing with finances that I believe happens with demonic deliverance. People are always looking for a get-rich-quick plan. Or they fall into the trap of thinking that everything is a devil and that if you can cast it out, everything will be better.

If that is the case, where is the personal responsibility? I believe God can deliver in one shot and snap of the finger. However, I believe this usually happens when we have shown we can be trusted with deliverance, healing, or financial breakthrough. Most people do not want to talk about that, but it is true.

I am starting with this because I believe a major transfer of wealth is scheduled. And right now, God is looking for a few good men and women that he can trust, not only with wealth but also with the wisdom and power to get wealth. I believe this revelation will truly challenge and change your life.

I was preparing to speak at a Telethon when God spoke this revelation to me. For the first time, I saw in the scripture what happens when you sow at the Thousand-Dollar level. There are so many people that do not believe this message, but I am writing to you from experience. I have emptied my bank account several times. I have sown from my personal account and ministry at the Thousand-Dollar level many times.

As a result, I have countless testimonies of where God blessed me and my ministry through the years.

If you are reading this book, it is because you desire to increase knowledge and revelation in seedtime and harvest. I believe there is an anointing in the earth for this transfer, and this is one of the revelations leading to it. I believe you are reading this because God has chosen you to learn more about this revelation that will lead to great breakthroughs in your life.

Read This Declaration
Over Your Mind and Life

I want to declare these truths over your life that from this day forward, the spirit of poverty and its mindset will never again have a place in your life. I declare that every lie and fallacy will be uprooted, and God will replace it with revelation and truth.

I speak over you that the revelation of these pages will come alive in your spirit and begin to lead and guide you into the inheritance that God has for you.

I declare that you will sow and give from a revelatory, heavenly mindset that will release the best of heaven's resources into your life. I declare that from this day forward, you will never give according to your resource but by faith in God as your source.

I declare that every debt will be canceled in your life and that business plans and ideas will come to you in the midnight hour. And that these ideas will create generational wealth in your life.

I declare that wisdom is yours and that you will operate in the wisdom that will break you through every line of the devil's defense. You will see your family saved, your body healed, your marriage blessed, and the treasures of darkness and hidden riches in secret places will be revealed and given to you.

I declare that every blessing, promise, and prophecy hovering over your life will be released as you apply the principles of this revelation.

Favor, provision, and promotion are yours. Wisdom, guidance, and direction are yours. Your delay is over; your denial is rebuked. Your season of NOW is released, and your best and most blessed days will ever be in front of you. All of this is yours because the hidden wisdom of God and the mind of Christ are your compasses from this day forward, forever and ever. Amen!

Part 1:

Understanding the Wisdom Seed

One

Miracle Territory

Have you ever wondered why God always waits until our backs are up against the wall, down to our last dollar, about to go bankrupt, lose our marriage and our minds, before He starts to move? I wished my timing and His were always on the same page. I have noticed in scripture that God's greatest miracles were worked in people in these conditions where you may be right now.

As you are reading this book, I want to make sure I encourage you. If you are in these conditions that I have just mentioned, take a moment right now and rejoice because you are in miracle territory. The Bible says in James 1 to count it all joy when we fall into various trials. Why is that? This is when God does His greatest work. However, it is difficult to grasp this reality in our finite minds.

Think about it, everyone loves a miracle, but who loves the tension and stress leading up to it? I know I do not. Whoever does, needs to write a book on the tension and stress of crisis and why I enjoy it.

Let us take a look at scripture; the man at the pool of Bethesda was there thirty-eight years before he received his miracle. Jesus then shows up and simply asks the man, "Do you want to be made whole?" Peter and his friends fished all night and caught nothing. They were washing their nets and about ready to go home, and then here comes Jesus. He has the audacity to tell him to launch out again and let down his nets for a catch.

Think about this momentarily; you pull an all-nighter and catch nothing but a can, a shoe, some seaweed, and a couple of old rags when Jesus says to go back out again. Are you kidding me? Did Jesus really ask me after pulling an all-nighter and catching nothing to try again? My thought would be, Jesus, I am exhausted. Why don't we try again some other time?

Let us consider the woman with the issue of blood. The Bible says she spent all she had and tried every doctor that money could buy. And by the time she was broke, she was worse off than when she started. At the end of this twelve-year journey, she is completely broke, busted, and disgusted, and suddenly, here comes Jesus.

The Bible says she hears that Jesus is passing by, and suddenly faith hits her heart. She rises up and says within herself, "If I may but touch the hem of His garment, I shall be made whole."

The difficulty of being in miracle territory is that most of the time, you are physically, mentally, spiritually, financially, and emotionally exhausted, and now God wants to give you a "suddenly" moment.

I know we all remember the story of Abraham and Sarah. Abraham was seventy-five years old and able to still have children when God gave them the promise. However, Sarah was unable to conceive at that time. I am sure they tried and tried and tried but to no avail.

Can you imagine how frustrating it must have been to have the ability to conceive, but God did not move? Then one day, after years of trying, Abraham developed a condition that required Viagra. However, there was none to be found. Talk about going from bad to worse.

At one point, Abraham had the ability and was waiting on God, but God never showed up, and now his body is dead. He cannot even try anymore. It is one thing to have a promise and the ability to try. It is another thing to have a promise and no idea or ability to bring it to fruition.

God waited until he was ninety-nine years old, twenty-four years after the promise, and said *next year, this time, you will have a son.* Why does God do that to us? It is because He knows how to get the glory. Whenever God is ready to bring a miracle into your life, He must wait until there is no way you can take credit for it. The reason for this is because He will not share His glory with anyone. He is God all by Himself.

Sarah's womb was closed, Abraham's body was dead, and they both were ninety-nine years old. They had no more strength to try. They could not have tried if they wanted to. They were well passed the years of fertility. This is when God does His best work. This is why you are where you are. God is ready to do a miracle in your life, and you are only one word away, one revelation away from the greatest breakthrough of your life.

I hope you are ready! Because even though you may have been sitting for thirty-eight years like the man at the Pool of Bethesda, or twelve years like the woman with the issue of blood, maybe you have fished all night and caught nothing, God has not forgotten about you, and wisdom is right around the corner.

Each one of the people that I just mentioned needed a miracle. Do you realize that each one of them only needed one word? That is all any of us need is one word from God. One wisdom instruction can change anything and everything in your life. Everything is about to change when God steps in and starts giving instructions.

You may have your back against the wall, but I want to encourage you to keep moving forward and reading on. I am about to help you unlock the greatest miracle of your life. All you need is one instruction of wisdom; everything in your life can be different. This is a time when you are a candidate for God to speak to you about the Wisdom Seed.

Two

$\longrightarrow\!\!\!\gg\!\!\gg\!\!\gg\!\!\gg\!\!\gg\;\;\lll\!\!\lll\!\!\longleftarrow$

Trials and Tribulations: The Prerequisite for the Wisdom of God

II Corinthians 4:7-9 *But we have this treasure in earthen vessels that the excellence of the power may be of God and not of us. We are hard-pressed on every side, yet not crushed; we are perplexed, but not in despair; persecuted, but not forsaken; struck down, but not destroyed.*

James 1:5 *If any of you lacks wisdom, let him ask of God, who gives to all liberally and without reproach, and it will be given him.*

This revelation that I am about to share with you came at a time when my Wife and I were one year into a blooming, pro-life pregnancy center. We were pastoring a church with no parking and badly needed a new building. Last, we were leading a pastors and business leaders fellowship that was growing as well.

Needless to say, I was feeling a little overwhelmed. Not with the work, because I have always been a hard worker, but I wanted wisdom and understanding on how to do the work and to make it grow. It was the first time in my life that I felt like, "Lord, I really need wisdom." I had a lot of things going, but I needed to know how to make them flourish and prosper.

Do you realize that God often uses trials, tribulations, obstacles, and hardships to position you for wisdom? Most people want God's glory and anointing but do not realize that you do not need it if you are not going through anything. The true prerequisite for God's wisdom is to be in a situation where you do not have wisdom and need it. The prerequisite for His strength is to be weak, and the prerequisite for His anointing is to be overwhelmed and have no ability in yourself.

Whenever you lack, God will pick up the slack. The only thing is that we must humble ourselves and ask in faith. God is such a good shepherd that when He sees His people struggling and lacking, He cannot deny Himself. He is moved by a person who asks for His help when they are lacking. The Bible says that Jesus was moved with compassion because they were like sheep having no shepherd. The 23rd Psalm says, "The Lord is my shepherd; I shall not want." One translation says, "The Lord is my shepherd; I shall lack for no good thing." This is because the shepherd's heart loves supplying your lack.

II Corinthians 4 talks about the treasure or the anointing within us. Do you realize that every time you go through a trial or difficulty or need wisdom, the treasure (the anointing) within you kicks in? This scripture has been a lifeline to me.

If you do not realize the purpose of the trials, setbacks, and tribulations, you will start thinking something is wrong instead of realizing you are right where God wants it to be. The effects of trials and tribulations on God's people activate the anointing within them. Do you realize that you are a candidate for wisdom when you are in a time when your life is void of it?

Never question God's love for you just because you are going through trials. The Bible says in the book of Romans what can separate us from the love of God? Neither death nor life, nor angels nor principalities nor powers, nor things present nor things to come, nor height nor depth, nor any other created thing, shall be able to separate us from the love of God which is in Christ Jesus our Lord.

It does not matter how high up you are or how low you are. Nothing can separate you from God's love. God's wisdom and strength are shown most effective when we are at a place of the greatest need for it.

The Bible also says in I Corinthians 10:13 that God will make a way of escape from every temptation. This is so encouraging because that means that in every trial and situation, you are never alone, and God will always have an answer to bring you out of whatever it is that you are in.

This is why we can count it all joy when we fall into various trials. When you read through James Chapter 1, you see that God wants to give us wisdom when we fall into these trials. God uses these trials and hardships to qualify us for His wisdom and grace. This is a hard saying, and it is difficult to receive. Our carnal nature and natural mind want it the easy way. However, we must ask ourselves this one question. How can I appreciate it if I do not see a need for it?

God refuses to create a life for you that makes Himself unnecessary. The only way you can value the anointing and wisdom of God is when you see your need for it.

You may be reading this book because you need to realize that you are in miracle territory but do not know how to identify it. It may be a ministry that needs God's touch, a spouse that has gone wayward, or maybe you need a financial breakthrough. Or maybe it is a child or grandchild that does not know the Lord, and you are desperate to see them come to know Jesus. Maybe you are in a situation where a decision needs to be made, and you are unsure what path to take. I may not have even mentioned it, but it really does not matter because God knows. Whatever it is, God has not forgotten about you, He has a plan for you, and there is wisdom for your breakthrough and next level. I believe you are exactly where God has called you to be. It may seem very hard right now, but God's wisdom and anointing are right around the corner.

You are in miracle territory as long as you do not give up. You are right where God has called you to be. You are being set up because God is ready to release wisdom into your life. I hope this chapter has helped you to see that you are not a lost cause. I hope you see that God have you set up and that His anointing and wisdom are available because of what you are going through. Remember that trials are not the end for us as believers; it is just the beginning. The treasure (the anointing) in you is scheduled to release the wisdom of God that will break you through every line of the devil's defense.

You have heard me mention the blessing of God's wisdom and that it is available for you and me. However, the question we must ask is, "What is Wisdom?" Once we understand wisdom, we can position ourselves to receive it when we sow the Wisdom Seed.

Three

————≫≫≫≫ ≪≪≪≪————

What is The Wisdom of God?

We must understand the whole process to appreciate the concept of a Wisdom Seed. My hope is that you would begin to understand the concept of when we are in miracle territory, how God sets us up for a miracle, and now what wisdom is and why we should desire it.

So, what exactly is this word wisdom, and why should we desire it? I am sure that you have heard someone say this person is very wise or that this person is full of wisdom. Here is another thought, why does God value wisdom so much, and what does the bible say about it? I want to take a moment and answer these questions, which are so important because it is very difficult to appreciate and value what you do not understand.

To start, let us look at what the dictionary says about wisdom. When I looked up the definition, this is what it says:

Wisdom: the quality of having experience, knowledge, and good judgment; the quality of being wise, the soundness of an action or decision with regard to the application of experience, knowledge, and good judgment; the body of knowledge and principles that develops within a specified society or period.

Let me narrow it down. Wisdom, simply put, is having the knowledge of knowing what to do, when to do it, and how to do it. I think back to that old saying that we all have said at some time or another, "If I had known then, what I know now, I would have done it differently." Ladies and Gentlemen, that is wisdom in a nutshell.

Many times, wisdom comes through the school of hard knocks. However, the Bible says in Isaiah 11:2 that there is a spirit of wisdom. Imagine having God's wisdom upon you and in you to make decisions. Obviously, God knows all things, and when His Spirit comes upon you, you have the mind of Christ to make good godly decisions. Let us look at a couple of scriptures on wisdom.

Deuteronomy 34:9 says that Joshua was full of the spirit of wisdom.

According to the scriptures, it says that Joshua was full of the spirit of wisdom. So, this lets us know that we can have a fullness of the spirit of wisdom as believers.

II Samuel 14:20 says that King David was wise, according to the wisdom of the angel of God, to know everything that is on the earth.

King David was wise, according to the wisdom of the angel of God, so he could know everything on Earth. This lets us know that wisdom gives us the ability to know what is on Earth.

> **Daniel 1:19,20** says that Daniel, Hananiah, Mishael, and Azariah had wisdom and understanding that was ten times better than the King's magicians and astrologers.

Daniel, Hananiah, Mishael, and Azariah (Shadrach, Meshach, and Abednego) had ten times more wisdom that was better than the King's magicians and astrologers. This lets us know that the wisdom of God is greater than any astrology, fortune-telling, or any other type of magic.

There are so many people that are looking for answers, such as, why am I here? What is my purpose? Why did this happen to me? All of these can be found in the wisdom of God. You do not have to look to any of the world or Satan's devices to find answers because God has wisdom just for you. All you must do is ask.

I am hearing more and more Christians looking to sorcery, astrology, and other types of fortune-telling to get answers. Do you realize that you may find some perverted form of an answer by looking at these? But it is important to note that using the devil's power for anything gives him access to your life.

This means that you may get answers, but then you might have a spirit of infirmity that you cannot get rid of. It could open a door that causes you to have unexplained tragic accidents or misfortunes. The devil never gives you anything without taking something from you. The Bible says that looking to these is an abomination to God. Never look to Satan and his powers to get answers that God will freely give to you from His love and His word.

Daniel and his friends had ten times more wisdom than any of the King's magicians or sorcerers, and this wisdom God wants to give you.

James 1:5 says, If we lack wisdom, we can ask God and He will give it to us liberally without reproach.

This lets us know that if we are in a trial and are looking for answers (wisdom), God will give them to us freely and without reproach. This means God will give it to you without any strings attached, unlike our adversary, the Devil.

Colossians 2:3 says, In Christ are hidden all the treasures of wisdom and knowledge.

The passage here in Colossians and so many others let us know that the wisdom of God is hidden in Christ Jesus. Remember, it is not hidden from you, it is hidden for you. If everyone had access to it, it would not be so valuable.

So many of God's chosen men and women were full of the spirit of wisdom. The Bible is very intentional about what it says and what it means. If God made it a point to make sure that the word wisdom was used to describe the characteristics of these men, then I believe we should pay attention to it.

The last one I want us to look at is Solomon. Let us see what the scriptures say in I Kings Chapter 4.

I Kings 4:29-34: *And God gave Solomon wisdom and exceedingly great understanding, and largeness of heart, even as the sand that is on the seashore. Thus Solomons' wisdom excelled over the wisdom of all the men of the East*

> *and all the wisdom of Egypt. For he was wiser than all*
> *men than Ethan the Ezrahite, and Heman, Chalcol, and*
> *Darda, the sons of Mahol; and his fame was in all the*
> *surrounding nations. He spoke three thousand proverbs,*
> *and his songs were one thousand and five. Also, he spoke of*
> *trees, from the cedar tree of Lebanon even to the hyssop that*
> *springs out of the wall; he spoke also of animals, of birds, of*
> *creeping things, and of fish. And men of all nations, from*
> *all the kings of the earth who had heard of his wisdom, came*
> *to hear the wisdom of Solomon.*

This book's concept is based on Solomon's life and the wisdom he received by sacrificing to God. Look at what he received. God gave him wisdom and understanding, along with an enlarged heart to comprehend the wisdom of God. His wisdom was so great that it excelled all the greatest philosophers and thinkers of his day. It says that Kings (not just mere men but leaders) came from all over the earth to hear Solomon's wisdom.

As a result of this wisdom, Solomon wrote over three thousand proverbs and wrote over one thousand songs. Not only did the wisdom of God cause him to write proverbs, but the man also became a songwriter. How many people talk about how they wrote or were inspired to write a song because of some experience they had? Solomon wrote from the spirit of wisdom God put upon him and the experiences God gave him.

This is why you do not need the spirit of the world, nor do you need to look to the world for what God has hidden in Christ Jesus. Let us go a little deeper and see how this wisdom impacted Solomon's life.

Wisdom and the Mind of Christ

In I Kings 3:16-28, it is the story of Solomon executing wisdom with two mothers. Both mothers had newborn babies, but one laid on her child and killed him in the middle of the night. When she found out her baby was dead, she went and switched her child with the other mother's living child in the middle of the night. When the other mother woke up, she knew the dead baby was not hers. Realizing that the baby was not her own, she brings the matter before the wise King Solomon.

They both said the living baby was their own when she brought the matter before the King. However, King Solomon, full of the spirit of wisdom, knew exactly what to do. He tells them to cut the baby in half and give half to one lady and the other half to the other. In Solomon's great wisdom, he knew the real mom would not want the baby to be cut in half.

So as the story tells us, the woman who was the real mom says no, let her have the baby. Do not cut him in half. However, the other woman, who was not the mom says let him be cut in half. Under the spirit of wisdom, King Solomon knew that the real mother would rather let the baby live, even if she could not raise the baby, than have the baby mutilated and murdered. So, under this anointing of wisdom, King Solomon saved the day and brought the truth to light.

What is interesting is that a few verses before, he was asking God for wisdom, but after God filled Him, we see him operating and making decisions far above his years and experience. This is what happens when we get wisdom. Our ability to make the right decisions at the right moment increases.

Christ knows all things, and when the spirit of wisdom comes to us, it gives us the ability to know what He knows.

The difference between the wisdom of the world and the wisdom of God is that God's wisdom goes far beyond our years, experience, and knowledge. God gives you His mind on matters in the form of revelation. That is so amazing! Has God ever given you wisdom in a supernatural way? It is one thing for you to learn from someone else or your own mistakes, but it is another thing for God to give you wisdom from His mind. Is this wisdom available to the believer? Of course! The mind of Christ is available to us all. We only need to learn how to unlock it and tap into it.

I Corinthians 2:16: *For who has known the mind of the Lord that he may instruct Him? But we have the mind of Christ.*

This scripture lets us know that we can tap into the mind of Christ. You might be saying what is so special about that? Allow me to be didactic for a moment. If Christ knows all things, then He knows the hearts of every person. He knows what is to come and the numbered hairs on your head. He knows where you lost your keys and where you lost your wallet. He knows everything that has happened to you and will happen to you.

So, if He gives you wisdom according to his omniscient, all-knowing mind, that would be invaluable. All God must do is give you a small amount of what He knows, and that can change everything in your life.

Did you know that God knows where every piece of gold is? Every diamond, every piece of silver, every oil and gas well, God knows exactly where they are. He also knows where every pearl is hidden, and since He knows all these things, you are one revelation from anything you will ever need.

Do you realize that any problem in your life, from the salvation of family members, a business launch, finding a spouse, stepping into ministry, or healing for your body, is locked up in the mind of Christ in the form of wisdom? Did you know that this is available to you? The purpose of this book is to help you tap into God's wisdom in the mind of Christ. The Bible calls this the hidden wisdom of God, which we will get into in a moment. But before we do, let us take a look at another facet of wisdom.

The Creative Power of Wisdom

The Bible says something unique: those filled with wisdom were given supernatural abilities outside of their own talents. The purpose of these supernatural abilities was to fulfill what God had put in their hearts.

Wisdom is not only knowledge and understanding, but it is also the ability to do. When God grants wisdom, He will also impart what is needed to perform it. For each person below whom we will read about, God gave them the ability to perform the wisdom He put within them.

Exodus 28:3 (KJV): *And thou shalt speak unto all that are wise hearted, whom I have filled with the spirit of wisdom, that they may make Aaron's garments to consecrate him, that he may minister unto Me in the priest's office.*

Exodus 31:3: *[God called Bezaleel] And I have filled him with the spirit of God, in wisdom, and in understanding, and in knowledge, and in all manner of workmanship,*

Exodus 31:6 (KJV): *And I, behold, I have given with him Aholiab, the son of Ahisamach, of the tribe of Dan: and in the hearts of all that are wise hearted I have put wisdom, that they may make all that I have commanded thee.*

Exodus 35:26 (KJV): *And all the women whose heart stirred them up in wisdom spun goats' hair.*

Exodus 35:31: *And He has filled him with the spirit of God, in wisdom, in understanding, and in knowledge, and in all manner of workmanship.*

Exodus 35:35 (KJV): *Them has He filled with wisdom of heart, to work all manner of work, of the engraver, and of the cunning workman, and of the embroiderer, in blue, and in purple, in scarlet, and in fine linen, and of the weaver, even of them that do any work, and of those that devise cunning work.*

Exodus 36:1 (KJV): *Then wrought Bezaleel and Aholiab, and every wise hearted man, in whom the LORD put wisdom and understanding to know how to work all manner of work for the service of the sanctuary, according to all that the LORD commanded.*

These scriptures let us know that wisdom gives us instruction and understanding and the ability and power to carry it out. This means that God will give us an idea or invention, and He will also give us the ability to do it. This means that if God gives you wisdom, within it also has everything you need to carry it out. Wisdom gave them all the ability to carry out and perform what God put in their heart to do. Do not worry about all the details. Everything you need is within the wisdom that God has revealed to you. As you step out, trust and obey what God has put within you; all the details will take care of themselves. This is the power of the hidden wisdom of God.

Everything you need is locked inside the hidden wisdom of God. Do not look for money, healing, or breakthrough. This is not wrong in itself. Ask God for wisdom. Are you ready for a phenomenal revelation? Here it is... **Wisdom is the means to a desired end.** This is why when people desire a healing, financial breakthrough, deliverance, etc. God gives an instruction. Those things are the ends that each one of us needs.

However, we must ask, how do we get to the desired end? It is the Wisdom of God hidden in the mind of Christ. This hidden wisdom is the vehicle that God uses to get us to the desired end that we want. God gives this to us in the form of instruction. The instruction of God's wisdom leads us to the fulfillment of the promise that we have asked of Him.

We see in the scriptures that when people would come to God and ask for a miracle, God never granted anyone a miracle without their participation. God wants a partnership and collaboration. Each time a person asks God for a miracle, He gives them a word of instruction (wisdom), and as they walk it out, their miracle comes to fruition. However, as we will see, the wisdom of God many times is foolishness to our natural minds.

Four

The Mystery of the Wisdom of God

B efore you read the next couple of chapters in this book, take a few minutes and read through I Corinthians Chapters 1:17- 2:16. These passages of scripture will help you to understand a deeper revelation of the next few chapters you are about to read. This is what this book is truly about. I want to share with you the revelation that God gave to me about tapping into this wisdom. I believe it is the key to obtaining the breakthrough that God has planned for your life.

> **I Corinthians 2:7,8**: *But we speak the wisdom of God in a mystery, the hidden wisdom which God ordained before the ages for our glory, which none of the rulers of this age knew: for had they known, they would not have crucified the Lord of glory.*

How is the wisdom of God a mystery? Simply put, it does not make any sense. Think about what you just read. If Satan had thought by crucifying Jesus he was sealing his own defeat and enabling God to redeem the world, he never would have done it. Jesus is suffering the most horrific death; meanwhile, Satan is losing. The whole time the devil thought he was winning, but in the wisdom of God, it was securing our salvation.

The Bible says in I Corinthians 1:18-29 that God uses the foolish things of the world to confound the wise and the weak things of the world to put to shame the things that are mighty. Simply put, God uses foolish means to bring about great miracles. God used the crucifying of His only Son to bring about the defeat of Satan and the redemption of humankind. God's means and instructions do not always make sense to our minds, but when they are followed in faith will yield the greatest of miracles. All things do not always have to make sense for them to be God.

Everything in the kingdom of God is the total opposite of the world. When the world says to live, God says die. When God says live, the world says die. The world will tell you to retaliate, but God says to love your enemies. The Bible says to give, and it shall be given, but the world says to take. I could go on and on, but you get the idea. Every time we put our faith in the wisdom of God and do it, it releases the miraculous power of the kingdom.

No wonder why Paul says to us in Romans Chapter 12 to renew our minds so we can prove the good, acceptable, and perfect will of God. This is simply because the wisdom of God is a mystery. It does not make sense to the natural mind, but it works.

God wants us to put our faith in His word and the results it brings, not what the world says we should do or how we should do it. Someone is reading right now that you have the right to divorce, but God may be leading you to stay. Someone is down to their last dollar, and God is talking to you about sowing. You might have just declared bankruptcy, but God is talking to you about going into business. All of this may seem crazy to the natural mind, but you must ask yourself, whose report will you believe?

This is the mystery of the wisdom of God. The world always wants it to align with our natural mind, and if it does not add up, it cannot be God. I have realized that true faith does not need the natural mind to be God. This reminds me of the statement I learned as a kid: "How can a brown cow chew green grass and produce white milk?" I am sure we all have probably heard that one, but think about it, isn't the mysterious wisdom of God the same way?

Let us look at some of the means that were used to work great miracles that seem crazy to the natural mind but worked for those that believed. Take some time to read the passages below in your own Bible to see how God uses His mysterious wisdom to work great miracles.

In **Exodus 14**, God tells Moses to part the Red Sea with a Rod.

In **I Kings 17:7-16**, Elijah tells a woman that was down to a little meal and oil before she was going to die to make him a cake first and then make for her family.

In **II Kings 5:1-19**, Elisha tells Naaman (a man with a skin disease) to go and dip in the nastiest river seven times, and he would be made whole.

> In **Mark 7:33**, Jesus put his fingers in a man's ears and spits on his tongue to heal a man that was deaf and dumb.

How many people do you know that would let you spit on their tongue to loosen their tongue to speak, especially in this COVID-19 world?

> In **John 9:7**, Jesus made mud from his spit and rubbed it in a man's eyes and told him to go wash in the pool of Siloam, and the man came back seeing.

There are so many more scriptures in the Bible of people that were given wisdom and instructions to bring about their miracles. Remember that God never uses the world's wisdom to accomplish His purposes. Most of the miracles in the Bible are almost irrational.

When you are truly walking by faith, God will often give you an instruction that does not make sense to the mind. You must know His voice and that you are hearing from Him. You must hear with the ear of faith and see with the eye of faith.

The reason why I wanted to take a moment and mention the mysterious wisdom of God is that it is also this way with the message of seed time and harvest. We will get into this in a moment, but doesn't the world say that this whole message of giving and seed time and harvest is nonsense? But if you have ever tried it, you know it works. If you do not believe in the mysterious wisdom of God and believe in it, then the message of the Wisdom Seed will seem foolish to the natural mind.

So, realizing all of this, what is the purpose of this hidden wisdom? It says in I Corinthians 1:29 that God uses these things so that no flesh can glory in His presence.

Five

The Hidden Wisdom of God

> **I Corinthians 2:6-10**: *However, we speak wisdom among those who are mature, yet not the wisdom of this age, nor of the rulers of this age, who are coming to nothing. But we speak the wisdom of God in a mystery, the hidden wisdom which God ordained before the ages for our glory, which none of the rulers of this age knew; for had they known, they would not have crucified the Lord of glory. But as it is written: "Eye has not seen, nor ear heard, Nor have entered into the heart of man The things which God has prepared for those who love Him." But God has revealed them to us through His Spirit.*

This scripture has totally changed the way I look at so many things. The first thing to realize is that it says we speak wisdom among mature people. This is important because you never give wisdom to those not mature enough to receive it. This is why God often has to process you and make you wait until your maturity level is ready to receive this wonderful, mysterious wisdom.

There are two facets of wisdom that we must consider. The first one is that it is a mystery, and the second is that it is hidden. The first one we dissected in the previous chapter. The second one we are going to dive into now.

If you think of a mystery movie or novel, a person must seek, pay the price, dig, and investigate until they solve the mystery. This is why it takes maturity to solve a mystery and to be a candidate for the Wisdom of God. If it does not come easy, immature people will quit at the first sign of resistance. They do not understand that anything that is valuable must be sought after, and a price must be paid to obtain it. This is also why God has it hidden; it is too valuable, and if you can be detoured from seeking it out, then you are not qualified to have it.

Do you realize that everything that is a valuable commodity on Earth is hidden? It does not matter whether it is gold, silver, pearls, diamonds, oil wells, etc. They are all very valuable, so God has them hidden. It is the wisdom of God to hide what is costly. So, we must understand that what is valuable has a price and must be searched for.

Proverbs 25:2: *It is the glory of God to conceal a matter, but the glory of kings is to search out a matter.*

If you think of any great teacher or educator, when they are educating, they give you enough to let you know there is the answer, but they do not give you all of it. A great educator understands that great wisdom has a price, and it must be searched for. They also realize that if you are not willing to search for it, you are not qualified and worthy to have it. They do this because they have paid the price for what they have.

I remember when I was first married. My mentor and I were having a conversation about how his marriage became so successful. I remember telling him I wanted a marriage like his one day. He responded, "Jay, you can have what I have when you have paid what I paid." Every person with wisdom understands that there is a price for it, and until someone wants to pay that price, it will remain hidden from them.

Let me start for a moment and talk to some hidden people out there. There may be someone wondering why they have not found a spouse yet. Or maybe a person that knows how valuable and gifted they are wondering why no one else sees them or has given them an opportunity. It is not that something is wrong with you, but you are more valuable than you know.

God has hidden you because you are special and valuable to Him. Do not forget, God always hides what is valuable. The Bible says in Proverbs 31, "Who can find a virtuous woman? Her price is far above rubies." Notice the words find, price, and rubies. Do you see the correlation? Anything valuable has a price and is not easily found. It must be sought out in order to be obtained.

That is why the Bible says, "He that finds a wife, finds a good thing and obtains favor from the Lord." Once again, notice the words finds, good thing, and favor. This shows us again that to find a good and valuable thing, it must be pursued. This is the price tag for the wisdom and favor of God. Can I go a little deeper with this?

Why does God allow what is valuable to be hidden? The purpose of being hidden is twofold. The first reason is that God wants what is hidden to accurately understand its value. I believe someone reading right now knows they have greatness within them but does not understand why they have not been discovered. I have learned that God wants you to understand your value, why you have value, and how to use what God has put within you before He reveals who you are to the world.

Sometimes God waits because if you do not know your value, you will sell yourself short and find yourself used and abused. He loves you too much for you to short-change yourself because you did not understand the greatness within yourself, and you were in a rush to be used. Be careful with going out of season; you might find yourself used and abused by the wrong people who see your value for selfish reasons.

The second reason is that someone out there needs to discover what God has hidden within you. However, they will have to dig until they find you. I am sure you are saying, but when is that? You must trust God until His sovereign mind says its time, and He allows you to be discovered by the discoverer. He has it all worked out, but you must trust His timing. The greater that something is, the more it must be processed and the deeper one must dig to obtain it.

God does some of His greatest work when people are in hiding. So, if you find yourself being hidden or seeking out what has been hidden, realize God has a purpose in the process, and His timing is perfect.

If God has you hidden, it is only because you are worth so much to Him. You are a prized possession, and He will not share you with just anybody. So, while God has you hidden, realize that you are very valuable, and He has a people that will truly value you and seek out what He has hidden within you.

The Bible says in Hebrews Chapter 12 that for the joy that was set before Jesus, He endured the cross and despised the shame. This means that Jesus saw beyond the cross, the pain, and the suffering and was willing to endure it because He saw the value on the other side.

Where did He get this understanding and this perspective? He received it when He prayed in the garden of Gethsemane. However, He did not pray once, not twice, but three times. It took Jesus three times in prayer until He saw the revelation on the other side. Now while the disciples were sleeping, He was praying and breaking through to the other side of the cross. My Lord, there is definitely a message in this! Think about how many people are sleeping on their purpose, breakthrough, and blessing while others are pressing in.

After Jesus prayed three times, He saw the wisdom and reward of going beyond the cross's shame, pain, and difficulty. This now brings us back to what we read earlier. If the prince of this world had known he was crucifying the Lord of glory, he never would have done it. This wisdom was hidden in the pain and difficulty of the cross.

How many people are rebuking and asking God to remove what is taking them to their next level in God? This is why we must ask God for wisdom when we hit hardships. All things are working together for your good. Not just some things but all things. Every time you hit a hardship, realize that wisdom is available for you. However, it is hidden in the trial. You must seek it out and ask God to reveal it to you.

So what keeps a person seeking out this wisdom, even when it is hidden? It is faith. When faith comes, it changes everything. What if Jesus had prayed only once or twice? Do you realize that by pressing in, it changes your perspective? The press is the perspective changer!

It is in Your Pressing that God Releases a Blessing

This is where what is hidden becomes revealed. This is where the pain and suffering make sense. This is where God shows you that it is worth it all. Truly, there is something that breaks and changes when people press in.

This is the revelation behind the wisdom that is hidden. It is only for those who understand its value and dig deep enough to find it, for it is in the press that our perspective is changed into the mind of Christ.

There may be someone right now that is saying, "If it is that hidden, how in the world will I ever be able to find it?" That is what makes it God and makes it faith. God gives you just enough faith to dig deep enough and long enough to see the hidden wisdom of God.

Faith refuses to be refused and denies to be denied. Faith keeps knocking until it reaches the purpose for which it was sent. The Bible says we are to ask and keep on asking, seek and keep on seeking, and knock and keep on knocking, and it will be opened. Notice the persistence. This is what it takes to get the wisdom of God. But this only happens when you tap into faith. Faith is what God grants you to dig deep enough and long enough to inherit the wisdom of God.

Six

Faith: The Currency for Wisdom

As a person who strongly believes in the message of seedtime and harvest, it bothers me when people ask, "Can you buy a miracle?" Of course not! Money is not the currency of heaven. Faith is! However, that does not mean that God cannot ask a person to use money as a vehicle to show their faith.

> **Hebrews 11:6**: *But without faith, it is impossible to please Him, for he who comes to God must believe that He is and that He is a rewarder of those who diligently seek Him.*
>
> **Romans 10:17**: *Faith comes by hearing and hearing by the word of God.*

Everything valuable has a price; anytime you purchase something, it requires a currency or payment method. If something has a price, it must have a method of payment. The greater the value, the greater the payment. We must realize that faith is the currency of heaven. To get the wisdom of God, you must have faith. The greater the wisdom, the greater the faith.

To have faith, you must be a believer in Jesus, and if you are a believer in Jesus, then faith is the gift of God that belongs to you so you can inherit the wisdom of God prepared for you.

This is why I say it is not hidden from you but for you. It would be common if it were out in the open for everyone to see (including unbelievers). Everyone would have it, and it would have no value. However, God has it hidden in the spirit realm where only those that are blood-washed and blood-bought have the heavenly currency of faith to obtain it. What a pleasure it is to have this privilege! You and I have the right to ask God for this wisdom, and He will give us the faith to obtain it. Let us read this scripture and move forward in this revelation.

I Corinthians 1:27: *But God has chosen the foolish things of the world to put to shame the wise, and God has chosen the weak things of the world to put to shame the things which are mighty; and the base things of the world and the things which are despised, God has chosen, and the thing which are not, to bring to nothing the things that are, that no flesh should glory in His presence.*

Interestingly, God takes the things that the world calls foolish to confound the wisdom of this world. Notice how there are different words alluding to the word wisdom in I Corinthians 1:27. Let us look again at the mysterious ways that God works miracles and how the world calls it foolish.

Think about how many miracles Jesus worked and how the religious zealots of the day tried to find something wrong with it. They said He should not be healing on the Sabbath, and He cast out devils by Beelzebub, is not this Joseph the Carpenters Son, and many other things. Meanwhile, people's lives were forever changed. The Bible shows where prophets, God, and even Jesus Himself used many different objects and methods to produce miracles. God used a rod with Moses, Elijah used a woman's meal and oil, and David used a slingshot and a stone. God can use anything as long as it is mixed with faith.

In another place, Jesus spits on a man's tongue, and it loosens him to be able to talk. I tell you what, if a preacher spits on my tongue, I better get healed in Jesus's name, or there may be problems.

Jesus told Peter to go fishing at a time that He needed to pay His taxes, and he brought up enough to pay for Jesus and his own. David went down to a stream of water and found five smooth stones and a slingshot to bring down the greatest warrior of their day. God told Noah to build an ark when there had never been rain before (let alone a flood), but He did it, and we see how it brought about salvation.

Why, then, does it take faith? Because if you look at the above examples, the natural mind will say you are a fool if you do that, but faith can receive it. Faith can believe that a rod can part the Red Sea. Faith can believe that a slingshot and a stone can kill Goliath. Faith says, 'Ok, Jesus, you can spit on the ground and make mud, wipe it in my eyes, and I will believe that I can receive my sight.'

It takes faith to operate in the wisdom of God. God does it like this, so our faith does not rest in a formula or the means but in the miraculous God we serve. That is why it is the currency of heaven that unlocks the wisdom of God. It was never the means to get to the miracle; it was faith in the miracle worker.

So, if God used these unusual means to work a miracle by faith, then it is by reason that we can believe that God could use money (seed time and harvest) to perpetuate a miracle in our lives if we believe. It is not the money, and it is not buying a miracle; it is putting our trust in God. It is believing Him, doing what He asks, and watching Him work. It is not in the money but faith in God.

In this generation, we see how many people have had issues with the message of seed time and harvest. But we must ask ourselves, If God used unusual means to work miracles in the past, why can't He use our finances the same way? This is the reality. God does use the message of seedtime and harvest to bring about miracles. However, it requires faith to do it.

I am personally convinced that it works. I am so convinced of giving, tithing, sowing, and reaping that even if it were not scriptural (which it is), I would still do it. But without faith, the message will not compute to the natural mind. It simply takes faith in God to bring about a miracle using this message. In the arena of faith, it really does not matter the means God uses to bring about the miracle. It just takes faith. God can use anything (including finances) if people can only believe.

The same way that a man needed to be healed from being blind, the lame to walk, and the 5000 to be fed is the same way that God can use money to bring miracles in our lives. It was very simple; they came to God asking for a miracle, and God gave them instructions, they obeyed, and their miracle was realized. So, we must ask ourselves this question, If God used those means back then, why can't He use money and the message of seedtime and harvest to do the same? The truth is, He can! It comes down to having the faith to believe.

You must realize that the moment God gives you a word, it has within it the potential to bring about what was promised. And, if you obey it, you will see that promise realized. The scripture says in Isaiah that God's word will not return to Him void but will accomplish what He sent it to do. The people that are obedient to the word of instruction by faith will start the process of their miracle the moment they obey.

When we start seeking God for a miracle, He may speak to us to use financial means, which the world says is crazy to do. However, do not forget that when the world says it is crazy, this is when God can do His greatest work. This is why I believe God uses money to bring about miracles when we hear and mix it with faith. God does this because the world says it should not be and cannot be done. It seems foolish to the world, but remember that He is still God. He can do anything He wants when He wants and how He wants.

Could it be, especially in America, the richest country in the world, that God would preach this message to us because we trust in our money more than Him? Could it be that even though our money says *In God We Trust,* maybe we do not as much as we should? Maybe this is why God uses it, so our faith will not rest in our money but in

Him who has blessed America to be as prosperous as she is. Just a thought, but I think it is worth mentioning.

I am sure that some out there would say that preachers have abused it, mishandled it, or manipulated it. I would say to you, of course there are. The devil always sends a counterfeit for whatever God is doing. There will always be someone that will try to mess up and pervert a good thing. So, let me insert this caveat.

I can guarantee that if you have gone out to eat more than a handful of times, someone or some restaurant gave you bad service, whether it was hair in the food, a poor waiter or waitress, a steak being cooked incorrectly, or anything you could imagine. How many people have said I will never go out to eat again because they had a bad experience? Now, you may not return to that exact restaurant, but I am sure most people will go out to eat again.

It is the same with churches, preachers, and the message of seedtime and harvest. Just because one person has perverted, it does not mean you should throw the baby out with the bath water, proverbially speaking.

What I am about to share is vital; every good preacher or teacher should be completely fine with it. This right here will free you from bondage, compulsive giving, manipulating preachers, etc. Are you ready? Here it is... ***You have to hear and know God for yourself!***

It is not as deep as you think. When a man or woman of God shares a word, your spirit has to judge that word, whether it is from God for you or not. I like to say it like this: your baby should leap within you about what is being said. I believe every word from a man or woman of God should be a confirmation, not just information. Never follow a word blindly. You should know God in a way that He confirms what is being spoken to you and not just following or listening to a man or woman apart from the Holy Spirit.

I love when Romans 8:15,16 says, "For you did not receive the spirit of bondage again to fear, but you received the Spirit of adoption by whom we cry out, "Abba, Father." The Spirit Himself bears witness with our spirit that we are children of God…"

When a man or woman of God shares what God is saying, you must ask yourself do you have the ear to hear at that moment? Is my Father bearing witness to what is being shared with me? Every word is not always for you, but you must try that word and see if God brings confirmation to your heart. If you are unsure, wait until you know, and then go and do it in faith.

The Bible says He that hath an ear, let him hear what the Spirit is saying. What does this mean? It means, is God speaking to you and calling you, and do you have faith in your heart to obey? This is very important. I have been in services and had money in my pocket, and the preacher would ask for a certain amount of people to give a certain amount. I am not saying they were not hearing from God, but I did not have faith in my heart to do it.

As a result, I did not give that time. However, there have been times when nobody may have heard what I was hearing, but I knew God was speaking to me. When I followed my heart and the faith I had to obey, I received my miracle.

When a word is spoken, because you are a child of God, God wants you to know His will. And if He wants to speak to you through someone else, His Spirit will bear witness with your spirit. So, at the end of the day, you are responsible for what you hear, how you judge what you hear, and what you choose to obey. If it is God, He will confirm. If it is not God, He will confirm that as well. But you must know God for yourself, and that is the key! You must be responsible for what you choose to obey.

If you follow the Holy Spirit in your life and allow Him to be the one to lead, guide, and direct, you will be fine. Do not allow a personality or your desire for a miracle to be the impetus for your faith. Allow the Holy Spirit to inspire you. Do not allow what others have said or will say about sowing to be the reasoning. Let faith and your relationship with God be the reason you follow a word or do not follow a word.

I believe you are reading this book because God does not want you to miss the greatest miracle of your life. I believe God wants to empower people to be financers of the gospel in these end times. I believe God wants to use you, but you cannot allow the doubters or what you have heard someone say negatively about this message to rob you of God's miraculous provision. Do not allow people who do not have faith concerning seed time and harvest or have not experienced it to negate and nullify what can change your life forever.

As we progress, I want to encourage you to taste and see for yourself. If you have been wondering, does this work? Or can it really be true? Ask the Lord to open your eyes so that you may see. You are His child, and He will lead you into all truth. He is not just God but your Daddy.

He loves you and wants what is best for you. He gave you His Holy Spirit to lead you into all truth, and you can know His voice and His will.

Last, remember, a man or woman with experience is never at mercy to a man or woman with an argument. God wants to give you a miracle of your own. And if He is impregnating your heart with faith, do not fight it, do not resist it, but follow it in faith. For if you do, you will see the miraculous provision of God in your life.

The word promises you that anything born of God overcomes the world. As we continue to move forward in this book, allow faith to fill your heart because that is where the miracle begins. Let us go now and learn about the revelation of the Wisdom Seed.

Part 2:

Activating the Wisdom Seed

Seven

Putting God First

II Chronicles 1:6-12: *And Solomon went up there to the bronze altar before the Lord, which was at the tabernacle of meeting, and offered a THOUSAND burnt offerings on it. On that night God appeared to Solomon and said to him, "Ask! What shall I give you?" Solomon said to God: "You have shown great mercy to David my father, and have made me king in his place. Now O Lord God, let Your promise to David my father be established, for You have made me king over a people like the dust of the earth in multitude. Now give me wisdom, and knowledge, that I may go out and come in before this people; for who can judge this great people of Yours?" Then God said to Solomon: "Because this was in your heart, and you have not asked for riches or wealth or honor or the life of your enemies, nor have you asked long life – but have asked wisdom and knowledge for yourself, that you may judge My people over whom I have made you king. Wisdom and knowledge are granted to you; and I will give you riches and wealth and honor, such as none of the kings have had who were before you, nor shall any after you have the like."*

If you look at this passage of scripture, it is evident that something happens at the Thousand-Dollar level in a believer's life. I have heard that spoken so many times and never quite knew what it was, even though I believed it. The previous chapters you have read have helped prepare you for what you are about to read now. They are foundational to helping you understand the seed time and harvest principle of the Wisdom Seed. So, let us summarize and explain how the process works.

Here are the principles we have previously reviewed.

1. **God puts you in miracle territory.** God often waits until your back is up against the wall, and people do not know where to turn. This is where God's wisdom is available for those who ask in faith.

2. **We ask God in faith to bring about a miracle.**

3. **God sends a word of instruction.** In faith, we turn to God to find a word of instruction. This word of instruction is the wisdom of God. These instructions can be foolish to the natural mind, but they will yield great results when obeyed. We have also discussed how God used a lot of unusual means, but as they were followed, God did great miracles. We also discussed how if God used those unusual means, why can't He use money as the means for a miracle?

4. **Our obedience to that word brings miracles and provision into our lives.** Our ability to follow this word of instruction releases God's provision and miracles in our lives.

I believe that every believer should try to get to a point where they can sow at that Thousand-Dollar level. This level is the place where the hidden wisdom of God is made known. Let us look at King Solomon.

King Solomon Kept God First

Have you ever heard someone say, "When I get it all together, I will come to God?" While it may seem very admirable to say that, it ultimately insults God. We must realize that we need God right from the start. If you are doing it yourself, you are working by the sweat of your own brow, which is part of the curse from the fall of Adam. God wants to work with you. He does not want you to do it on your own. Even when it comes to sowing and reaping, people always say, "When I get it, I will give it." However, this means it is about you, your ability, and your resources. The wisdom way is, God, I will start with You, and I know You will multiply it and use it for Your honor and glory.

When you keep God first in your life, all you have is not all you have. There is so much more. God wants to take the lid off what you have, but you must keep Him first and center. It is time for you to transition from your resources to God becoming your source. You can do this by keeping God first and obeying Him with what you have. God is the only Lord where obedience is paramount.

The story of King Solomon is where this revelation comes from. Solomon had come to power as king and was unsure of what he had within himself and decided the first thing he would do was to sacrifice and give to God.

If more people understood that, how much further along would we be?

As a pastor, I see so many people who fit God in where they can instead of making Him number one. When you are down to your last, do not have enough, and are not sure where to go, that is the time to make God first.

The Bible says in Matthew 6:33, "Seek ye first the Kingdom of God and His righteousness, and all these things will be added to you." Notice that "all these things will be added" is after we seek FIRST the KINGDOM and God's righteousness (His way of doing things).

This reminds me of the story in Luke 10:38-42 which recalls the story of Mary and Martha. If you have ever investigated this story, it really shows us the power of keeping God number one and at the center of all things.

Martha is distracted (which leads to frustration) with much serving. She then goes to Jesus and says, "Lord, do you not care that my sister has left me to serve alone? Tell her to help me."

Jesus responded to her: "Martha, you are **troubled** and **anxious** about **many things,** but **one thing** is **needed**, and Mary has chosen that good part, which will not be taken away from her."

Notice that she was distracted from what was most important: to keep God first and at the center. If we choose to keep God first, all these things will be added. When things are out of order, and we start with what we think is more important than God, anxiety and distraction will rule the day. Then you will have to work by the sweat of your own brow. This will affect you financially, maritally, ministerially, and in any and every area of your life. However, we are discussing seed time and harvest, so let us look at a biblical financial example.

I Kings 17—The Widow Woman at Zarephath

Elijah meets up with the Widow Woman of Zarephath (I Kings 17), and she has a little bit of oil and a meal. She is about to prepare this for her and her son and prepare to die. However, Elijah comes along and tells her, "Bake me a cake first." She says, "I don't have a cake but just a little meal and oil that I will prepare, and then we are going to die." However, Elijah gives her a word and says if you bake me a cake first, the oil and meal will not run out until the drought ends.

So, in the midst of her trial, which would lead to her and her son's death, God says (through Elijah), "Bake me a cake first." We must understand the power of keeping God at the center and keeping Him first in all that we do. It could have been very easy for her to say "NO!" Who could blame her? She only had enough for her and her son, and they will die. She could easily have eaten her seed. However, she does not do that; she starts with God.

Wherever you start with God, God begins. Every person must come to a point in their life where they realize that God is Alpha and Omega. He is the beginning and the end. However, most people think of just the beginning and end, but He is not just the beginning and the end; He is everything in between. Wherever you start with God, He will bless it from that point.

Let us decide right now to keep God first and always start with Him. As a result of her willingness to obey the Man of God's word, she and her household ate all the way through the drought, and everyone in her house was preserved.

Remember the story of Jesus multiplying the loaves and fishes and feeding the five thousand (not including women and children, which would probably mean it was around 8000)?

They did not have enough to feed the multitudes of people, but what did they do? They started with Jesus and brought the loaves and fishes to Him to put them in His hands.

This is what started Solomon on the right track. He started with God! The first revelation of the Wisdom seed is to remember to start with God. It does not matter how little you have. Little is much when God is in it. The first point of wisdom is simply starting with God.

Eight

Thousand-Dollar Level

Something happens at the Thousand-Dollar level. What is it? Why do preachers and teachers all over say it? It is because something really does happen. It is shown in the life of Solomon, and I want to share with you what the Lord shared with me for you.

The Thousand-Dollar level unlocks the hidden things of God. The Bible says in many places that God has hidden and secret things. Let us look at one of them now.

> **Isaiah 45:1-3**: *Thus says the Lord to His anointed, to Cyrus, whose right hand I have held – To subdue nations before him and loose the armor of kings, to open before him the double doors, so that the gates will not be shut. I will go before you and make the crooked places straight; I will break in pieces the gates of bronze and cut the bars of iron. I will give to you the treasures of darkness and hidden riches of secret places.*

When Solomon gave God the 1000 bullocks, it is amazing that He asked for wisdom. When he asked for it, God also gave him three other things. However, it is the only place in scripture where a person sows something at the Thousand-Dollar level, and we see a major response from God. God says to Solomon, "What do you want?" What an amazing thing to see the God of the universe ask someone, what do you want? It happened after he sacrificed 1000 bullocks.

I believe God allowed that to happen because, in His sovereignty, He knew what Solomon would ultimately ask for and wanted it to be a revelatory example. It is important to note that Solomon did not ask for anything but wisdom. And as a result, God gave him everything else.

The Bible says that because he did not ask for long life, the life of his enemies, or riches, God granted him wisdom and the other three as well. The Lord showed me that the three things (long life, riches, and the life of your enemies) are wrapped up in the spirit of wisdom. If you can get wisdom, you will get other things as well.

When a person gives to God at the Thousand-Dollar level, God gives them a spirit of wisdom so that they get a portion of the other three blessings (long life, riches, and victory over their enemy) as well. It could be one or all three.

The Bible says that the wisdom of God is hidden in a mystery. So when we sow at this level, it releases this hidden wisdom of God to us. This wisdom has always been there, but when we give to God at this level, it releases what God has hidden for us, to us. The way God gives this to us is by revelation. He shows us the things He has prepared for us and releases them to us.

When we sow at this level, it releases the treasures of darkness and hidden riches in secret places. Do you realize that you may be one seed away from revelatory wisdom? The Bible says that God has prepared hidden wisdom and predestined us to receive it from the foundations of the world (I Corinthians 2:7).

When a person sows at that level, it releases the spirit of wisdom that Solomon had upon their lives. This wisdom can be packed with long life, victory over our enemies, and riches. That means that when you and I sow, God will give us a spirit of wisdom that opens the door to divine revelation. That is why it is called the Wisdom Seed.

You are one revelation away from the greatest breakthrough of your life. I believe that God can use our faith to sow as a means to a miracle. The Thousand-Dollar level brings a spirit of wisdom, knowledge, and revelation. This revelation can come through a dream, an idea, or even an invention.

Proverbs 8:12 (KJV): *I wisdom dwell with prudence and find out knowledge of witty inventions.*

When wisdom comes upon you, anything can happen. You could have dreams, ideas, or anything that God wants to do. However, we must not forget it is after we have received the wisdom of God.

Interestingly, after Solomon sacrificed the one thousand bullocks, God showed up to him at night. Could that be in the form of dreams, waking you up at two or three in the morning with an idea? Yes, I believe God can give you dreams and ideas that will unlock the wisdom of God in your life and bring a miracle to your world. I believe these are the things we can and should expect from God when we sow at the Thousand-Dollar level. Something breaks and changes in the realm of wisdom whenever we sow to God in this dimension.

The first time I ever started preaching the wisdom seed, there was a person believing God for a new job, spouse, and a raise in their salary. After hearing this revelation, this person sowed that Thousand-Dollar seed, and as soon as they did, within the year, God relocated them to a better job, better pay, and better climate, and they found their spouse. It had always been there, but the wisdom seed broke it through.

If you remember, when I started the book, I stated how I needed the wisdom of God in ministry and needed some things to happen. We sowed a thousand personally and ministerially, and God opened up a dream opportunity for a new building that we are in now that we could not have afforded. But remember, favor removes the labor. When we sowed, God began to give us favor. We had a pastor that said God told him to help us, and he did. I did not even ask for it; the favor came and found me. Our ministry has grown tremendously with this move, and we have expanded like we have believed God for. That happened after we sowed the wisdom seed.

There are things that are hidden (yet already prepared) for you. They are in the mind of God, and when you sow at that Thousand-Dollar level, they are revealed to you. This is the hidden wisdom level. People may say that is crazy, and I would say to them, that is exactly what the Bible says you would say. I Corinthians 1:26-29 says that God uses what the world calls foolish to bring to nothing that the world calls wise so that no flesh can glory in His presence. I am not telling you something that has not been proven. Many people have said that something happens at the Thousand-Dollar level. This is the revelation of what it is.

This is why I took so much time at the beginning of the book to lay this revelation out. I wanted you to see how it comes to fruition. The fact is that when your back is up against the wall and you follow God's word of instruction, that wisdom releases the supernatural blessing and provision of God into our lives.

Remember, God can use any means He wants, and He does. It is not just money. It has definitely been proven that God can and will use our giving to bring about miracles.

Nine

Four Blessings of the Wisdom Seed

In this chapter, we want to look at the four blessings that come because of the Wisdom Seed. When you sow, these are things that I believe you should look for and will come to manifestation. There may be others, but I believe these are the four that happen in some shape or form each time a person sows at this level.

I want to also encourage you to look for these as you sow. Sometimes it happens very fast, and sometimes it takes time. But you will always see the goodness of the Lord in your life. I believe we need to expect and watch for God to move when we step out in faith.

Just like a Pregnant Woman

She knows the signs and what to look for as the birth of her baby approaches. And just like the birthing of a baby revolves around seedtime and harvest, so does the Wisdom Seed.

Let us look at these four blessings that we should be cognizant of and look for that come upon us when we sow at the Thousand-Dollar level. The first one is the Spirit of Wisdom.

The Spirit of Wisdom: A Perspective Changer

The first thing that comes upon you is the same thing that came upon Solomon… Wisdom. God gave Solomon supernatural wisdom beyond his years or his experience. When you and I sow, God gives us a spirit of wisdom beyond our own ability. Luke 4:18 says, "The Spirit of the Lord is upon me, for He has anointed me." Wow! Do you see that? When the anointing comes, everything changes. When we sow, the anointing of wisdom and favor comes upon us for service. The Spirit of Wisdom comes to give us a measure of the mind of Christ, and when we have his mind, everything changes.

Wisdom is knowing what to do, when to do it, and how to do what God has called us to do. Also, wisdom is the right perspective as well. When wisdom comes, it changes how we view a thing. Many people may be in a difficult spot, but when the spirit of wisdom comes and God changes their perspective, everything changes. Once a person sows, I believe it opens the eyes of their heart to begin to see their circumstance through God's perspective.

If you remember the story when Jesus fed the 5000 with five loaves and two fish, they did not have enough. His disciple's perspective said, "Lord, what are these five loaves and two fish among so many?" In the natural, that totally makes sense. If you look at it from that standpoint, that is nowhere near enough. However, when the Spirit of Wisdom comes (knowing what to do, how to do it, and when to do what God has called you to do), you get a different lens through which to view your circumstance, which changes everything.

Jesus operating under the Spirit of Wisdom, had a different perspective about the few loaves and fishes. He then gave an instruction that, when followed, gave them more than enough to feed everyone, with twelve baskets left over. It is important to notice that the wisdom instruction had to be followed to bring about the needed results.

The disciples saw it one way; Jesus, under the Spirit of Wisdom, saw it another. So, we can see that when the Spirit of Wisdom comes, one heavenly perspective shift can change everything. This is what the wisdom seed produces. It releases an anointing of wisdom to give you God's plan on how to work a miracle in your current circumstance.

Everything you need is already in you or around you. However, when God's perspective and reality are given to you, it can change how you see what you have. How many times in scripture do we see God say, "Lift up your eyes?" That simply means, put your eyes on Me and get my perspective. You might see what you have as insignificant, not enough, or a bust, but in God's hands and through His perspective, you have more than enough. As you sow, begin to ask God to open your eyes. Begin to look for God to change your perspective and realize everything you need is within you and around you.

When we sow at this level, God allows us to see what is in our house His way, and when we do that, our miracle begins. God is about to show you how to use what you have, which may be little, to bring about great results. This is the first blessing of the Wisdom Seed.

The Spirit of Revelation: Revelatory Keys

After the Spirit of Wisdom comes upon us, we can receive the second. The second blessing is Revelation (**Revelatory Keys**). When the Spirit of Wisdom comes upon us, we receive revelation, and with revelation comes revelatory keys. Revelatory keys *are heavenly knowledge and wisdom that open doors and give direction, provision, favor, and blessing to break you through every line of Satan's defense.*

Let us look at this passage to see how these revelatory keys bring blessings into our lives.

> **Isaiah 45:1-3**: *Thus says the Lord to His anointed, to Cyrus, whose right hand I have held – To subdue nations before him and loose the armor of kings, to open before him the double doors, so that the gates will not be shut. I will go before you and make the crooked places straight; I will break in pieces the gates of bronze and cut the bars of iron. I will give to you the treasures of darkness and hidden riches of secret places.*

This scripture reveals to God's people how He wants to give them the treasures of darkness and the hidden riches of secret places. To understand the purpose of these verses, you must first understand the beginning verses (V.1, 2) to understand how He brings about the end (V.3) treasures of darkness and hidden riches in secret places).

There are four different blessings from the Wisdom Seed. This is the second one broken up into four parts. Revelation is what gives us authority. Authority is the right to act or the authorization for one to act. The revelatory wisdom of God that comes from our obedience to God's word gives us authority.

In Isaiah 45:1-3, the Lord says to His anointed to go and subdue nations, open the double doors, make the crooked places straight, and break the gates of bronze and cut the bars of iron. This verse means there are things that are locked up by the enemy that God is authorizing His people to go and take.

When God gives you His hidden wisdom in the form of revelation, He gives you His authority. When He gives you wisdom, He gives you keys. Keys are a form of authority. Keys are the way by which we grant access. Keys are symbolic of authorization. This means that when you get a revelation from God, everything you need to subdue what God has given you has already been granted.

That means that every enemy, every door, every path, every gate, and every bar cannot stop what God has given you to do. This is what the wisdom of God gives to you as a believer. Nothing can stop you if you follow the instruction of the Lord. This is what comes upon a person that sows at the Thousand-Dollar level.

The treasures of darkness and hidden riches in secret places are the results of God's wisdom. His revelatory wisdom gives you the authority to subdue nations, open the double doors, make straight, crooked paths, and break the gates of bronze and bars of iron.

When God gives you revelation, you have everything you will ever need to carry out and see the promise manifest. When God gives you revelation, you get grace, favor, and provision (which we will go into more about later).

Grace: This is God's strength, made perfect in every weak area of your life.

Favor: Favor is when God works for you. I have heard it said like this: "Favor removes the labor." Favor is when God gives you promotions you did not deserve, blessings you did not pay for, and more. God will give you His favor to fulfill and walk out His purposes. God never gives favor where there is no need for the Kingdom to be advanced. The purpose of favor is to help you bring into manifestation the purposes of God.

Provision: I believe God is a God that pays for what he orders. When God gives you a word of instruction, you follow it. Provision is already packed inside the revelation.

Once you have received revelation, you only need to obey. When you need a miracle, faith comes in the form of revelation. God simply opens your eyes to what He has already prepared; all you must do is step out and receive it.

If you remember, when Peter got the revelation that Jesus was the Christ, what did Jesus say to Him? Let us read it.

Matthew 16:17-19: *Jesus answered and said to him, "Blessed are you, Simon Bar-Jonah, for flesh and blood has not revealed this unto you, but My Father who is in heaven. And I say to you that you are Peter, and on this rock, I will build my church, and the gates of hell shall not prevail against it. And I will give you the Keys of the kingdom of heaven, and whatever you vid on earth will be bound in heaven, and whatever you loose on earth will be loosed in heaven."*

Through this passage of scripture, we see that Peter gets revelatory wisdom from heaven.

Jesus says that flesh and blood did not give it to him, but the Father did. As a result, Peter was authorized and granted access because of the revelatory wisdom of God. Jesus said, "I will give you the keys to the kingdom." He also told him what he bound on earth would be bound in heaven, and what he loosed on earth would be loosed in heaven. Furthermore, Jesus told him that because of these keys, the gates of hell would not prevail against him. Wow! All of this is because of the revelatory wisdom of God released from the Wisdom Seed.

This is the second blessing you need to look for from the Wisdom Seed. It is the revelation that gives you authority or the right to act. God's word revealed to you in the form of wisdom gives you the right to have everything that God has promised to you.

When something is revealed, it means to show or make known what was already there. This is why it says in…

> **I Corinthians 2:9,10**: *But as it is written: Eye has not seen, nor ear heard, neither has it entered into the heart of man, the things God has prepared for those that love Him. But God has revealed them unto us through His Spirit.*

The Wisdom Seed (when we sow it in faith) allows the Spirit of Wisdom to reveal the hidden things to us that have been prepared for us. This is why sometimes, when your back is up against the wall, and all hell is breaking loose, it is actually a setup for God to give you revelatory keys. These keys are used to give you the authority to unlock and give you what you have been praying and believing for.

This is crucial for every believer to know. Why is that? Because Jesus came to give us back the dominion and authority that Adam lost in the garden. These revelatory keys, which come from the Spirit of Wisdom, guarantee we can have what God has already prepared.

The keys are the heavenly authoritative documents that we use on earth that prove to Satan and all of hell that we have the authority to take what God said is ours. These Rhema documents (inspired words from God) prove that God has given us the authority to bind and lose anything that stands in the way of what God's word has promised. It is amazing that this passage in Matthew 16 is the only place where it says the gates of hell will not prevail.

The Bible says, in **Isaiah 45:1, 2,** *that God will open before him the double doors so that the gates will not be shut, and I will break in pieces the gates of bronze and cut the bars of iron.*

When we get revelatory keys, things that have been closed off, doors that have been shut, must come open. This is why when people give at this level, things begin to supernaturally break open for them.

The Wisdom Seed releases authoritative heavenly keys to open what has been closed off to you. Think about it for a moment. What are keys for? To grant access. If I were to give you a key to anything I have (home, car, building, safe, etc.), it implies you have the authority or the right to access it.

The Wisdom Seed is one of the ways God grants you access to what seems to be closed off to you. All this happens because of Verse 3. God said he would give you the treasures of darkness and hidden riches of secret places. If it is hidden and a secret, it must be revealed and illuminated.

The Spirit of Wisdom gives us these revelatory keys when we sow in faith the Wisdom Seed to access these promises.

Now, that does not mean you must sow a thousand dollars every time to get this. Or that sowing is the only way to get this. Remember what we have discussed earlier, God uses many ways and means to bring about a miracle, and sometimes He uses our financial means to do so. That is one of the purposes of this book to debunk the fact that God cannot use our money to bring about a miracle. Or that it is only about preachers trying to get your money.

Despite all this, we must realize that there are times when God uses our finances to bring about a miracle, especially when we sow at the Thousand-Dollar level.

When we give at this level, the same spirit of wisdom comes upon us that came upon Solomon. And with that wisdom, God grants other things with it as well. Remember this: some things cannot be explained; they must be experienced. You might not understand some laws 100 percent, but they still work. I might be unable to explain the exact formula for gravity, but I know it works.

If you are sowing or deciding to sow at this level, you can probably say or will say the same thing. "I may not know the exact formula, but I know it works." Taste and see that the Lord is good.

When you have faith in God, He will send revelation for you to unlock what He has already prepared for you. This revelation is the wisdom of God given to you to deliver you out of whatever you are in. Another way of putting it, it is the next step in your life, it is the change to your diet that you need to get your health back, it is the direction you will follow to see your marriage healed or your family saved, and yes, it very well could be the financial breakthrough you are looking for.

Revelation changes everything. Revelation is the wisdom of God revealed to you. Revelation is the divine instruction packed with grace, power, ability, authority, and breakthrough to help you obtain the promises God has already prepared for you.

Divine Direction

> **Isaiah 45:2**: *I will go before you and make the crooked places straight.*

Let us now look at the third blessing of the Wisdom Seed. The third blessing is **Divine Direction.**

Have you ever seen someone with a metal detector at a beach or in the woods? I know I have. What are they looking for? They are looking for riches or valuables. The purpose of the metal detector is to let them know there is something beneath the ground that cannot be seen with the physical eye, but it is there. Once the detector detects the metal, the person must dig to find what the detector revealed.

There are a lot of people out there walking around, hoping to find something. They might even have a metal detector, but they are not sure where the goods are. Even with the detector, they may still be uncertain if the goods are where they are walking. They might even pick up a detection, but it could be an old can, a rusty old nail, or some other non-valuable item.

But what if I could tell you where the valuable goods were? You will still need to use your detector, and you will still have to dig, but there would be so much less effort needed. When you sow the Wisdom Seed, God gives you wisdom, and with wisdom comes divine direction to put you into position for the blessing you desire.

With wisdom, God positions you in the right place, where you may still have to search and dig, but you are near valuable goods. All you must do is put in the work, and God has already done the rest. He already knows where your breakthrough is, your building, your spouse, your finances, etc. You just need His wisdom. He hid it for you, and He is the only one that can reveal it to you. He can show you where everything you will ever need or want is.

Remember, God is not creating anything new. Everything that the world has ever needed is already on the earth. The Tesla you see today was already on the earth when He created the garden. The computer I was typing on at the time I of writing this book was in the garden. The TV you watch, your iPhone, your microwave, the list goes on and on and on, all of it was in the garden.

That means you and I are only one revelation away from discovery. We just need God to show us where to start digging, and we will be able to find what was already created and prepared for us before the foundation of the world.

Everything that you need right now is already in or on the earth. However, it would take a long time for you to search this whole earth. God already has it and knows where it is. When you sow in obedience to God, God gives you wisdom on where to start searching. God will even move you and position you in the right place to find it.

I remember the first time I ever sowed a Wisdom Seed. I was a young man in ministry, and I sowed a Wisdom Seed when I believed in God for a home. After I sowed it, the Holy Spirit directed me to call a lady that was a former member of my church and ask her what she was doing with her home because she had moved to Florida. Long story short, I ended up getting that home for $5000. It needed a lot of work, which God provided to do. He sent me workers to finish that home, and that set me up for my next home. By the time the miracle was finished, I had ended up owning the home of the guy who worked for me on my first home.

What is amazing is that my first home was very modest, and while this guy was working on my home, he took me through his house. I was so amazed at his house, and I loved it. It had six bedrooms, a two-car garage, a paved driveway, a full basement, and even a hot tub room.

Now, these were his exact words to me, "Pastor, maybe one day you will have a home like this." Needless to say, I own that home today and collect rent on it every month.

I am sure you are wondering; How did I get the home? Divine direction! The Bible says the footsteps of a good man are ordered by the Lord. I was counseling one day, and a guy came to my office and said did you hear that "so and so" was going to lose their home? I said, "No, I didn't know that." Needless to say, I got on the phone, and I ended up getting the house for $35,000, and guess what? The work needed to be done on that house, and the guy that said, "One day you might have a house like this." was the one that ended up doing the work for me. He ended up working for me to remodel his old house, which was now mine. Only God could do something like that. This was all because of the Wisdom Seed.

All of that happened because I sowed a Wisdom Seed, and God placed me in the right place at the right time to be positioned for blessing. If I had not sowed that, I would never have called the former member of my church, and I would have been out of position to get the house I really wanted. God knew all along what was happening and what was going to happen. It was hidden, but He revealed it to me, and I am blessed today because of His wisdom. That is divine direction. All of that came from a Wisdom Seed.

The Bible says in Isaiah 45:2 that God will go before us and make the crooked places straight. As you can see, that happened to me, and God wants to do the same for you. If He did it for me, He would do it for you. He is not a respecter of persons, and you can receive the same blessing. All you must do is be obedient to God in a seedtime, and the Wisdom Seed will do the rest.

Favor: Provision and Promotion

The last one of the four blessings of the Wisdom Seed is **Favor**. This favor comes in the form of provision and promotion. Let us look at a couple of scriptures as we look at how favor comes into our life through the Wisdom Seed.

Isaiah 54:3: *I will give you the treasures of darkness and hidden riches of secret places.*

I Corinthians 2:6,9,10: *But we speak the wisdom of God in a mystery, the hidden wisdom which God ordained before the ages for our glory. But as it is written: Eye has not seen, nor ear heard, neither has it entered into the heart of man the things which God has prepared for those who love Him. But God has revealed them unto us through His Spirit.*

I want to recap something just before our last point is revealed. Remember, the wisdom of God is hidden. When we sow in faith and follow the direction of God, He reveals to us the hidden things. Or in other words, He allows us to see and know the wisdom of God. It is shown here in I Corinthians Chapter 2. When Solomon sacrificed the 1000 bullocks, it released the Spirit of Wisdom, and God allowed Him to see what was hidden. Now, let us look at the fourth and last blessing of the Wisdom Seed.

The fourth blessing of the Wisdom Seed is favor in the form of provision and promotion. Now provision is not just limited to money but includes it. After the Spirit of Wisdom comes upon you, you receive revelatory keys and divine direction.

As a result, favor, provision, and promotion are inevitable. If God gives you His wisdom, revelation, and direction, how can you not have favor and be promoted and provided for? It is a package deal that comes with the Wisdom Seed.

Look at the Life of Solomon. After he received the Spirit of Wisdom, everything in his life prospered like never before. He made great decisions, his discernment went up, he became very rich, and Solomon had everything God promised. He also had a long life and victory over his enemies. Solomon made many good decisions and was blessed beyond measure due to the wisdom he obtained from the 1000 bullocks he sacrificed to God.

How many of us are still reading and benefiting from his writings thousands of years later because of His willingness to sacrifice at the Thousand-Dollar level? Let us not get it twisted; he received all of this after he sacrificed at the Thousand-Dollar level. He did not pray or fast; he sacrificed to God, and it released the blessing into His life.

There are a lot of ways that God sends His provision. Sometimes it comes in the form of a business idea or an invention. It may come in the release from God to start a ministry or to go back to school. There may be someone out there that believes in God for a spouse or home, and He is about to give you a lead on where to find it.

Proverbs 8:12 says that wisdom dwells with prudence and finds out knowledge and witty inventions. Why is this important? If God just gives you money, after a while, that will come to an end. But if God gives you a promotion, a business idea, or an invention, it can become exponential. It can even lead to generational wealth.

Do not get me wrong, if God blesses me with finances, I will receive it. But a business idea, a promotion, or an opportunity could lead to much more if it is stewarded correctly. The opportunities could be truly endless. My prayer for you is, "Lord, give them an idea and the favor or finances to bring it to fruition." I believe that when God gives you money, it is often because He is giving you the finances to start funding the idea He has given you.

It takes wisdom to understand this. When God gives you an idea or a witty invention, do not sleep on your idea. Kingdom ideas may come in seed form. You have to develop and process them, but everything needed is hidden within your ideas in a seed form. All you have to do is work on your seed (idea).

Get up and begin to work on what God has given you. Sometimes your harvest is the ideas God has given you and what they can generate. Remember, everything in the kingdom revolves around seed time and harvest, including ideas. I believe many times that when God gives you a harvest, it comes in the form of an idea.

Then God will give you financial favor to get it started. Become an investor and do not waste or eat your seed. God is giving you the funds and ideas to fund your idea, not just to spend on riotous living. He wants to see if you will be a good steward and invest or if you will just eat your seed.

If you do not steward what God has given you correctly, the harvest cannot be realized. Start working today on the idea God has given you, and use what you have to start developing what God has placed within you.

Sometimes your harvest will come in the form of a promotion. When we get a promotion, it usually comes with an annual raise in our salary. The question we have to ask ourselves is, what will we do with the increase? We must take the increase, invest it, and multiply what God has given us.

It is important not to consume your potential on foolish spending. Many times, God gives the financial increase, and people go into more debt and are worse off than they were before.

Also, with every promotion comes wisdom, education, and empowerment. Because with every new door comes an opportunity to learn and grow. As we steward this well, it can lead to another promotion. Sometimes the promotion you get is really meant to be a seed to develop into a greater harvest.

As you steward the promotion, you grow, and so do your finances, knowledge, wisdom, and the possibilities of greater levels of promotion. God is a God that takes us from glory to glory. However, the next level is always attached to how well we steward our current level.

When you are sowing the Wisdom Seed, look for God to give you promotion and opportunity. A scripture that comes to mind is Deuteronomy 8:18, "And you shall remember the Lord your God, for it is He who gives you the power to get wealth, that He may establish His covenant which swore to your fathers, as it is this day."

The Wisdom Seed releases the power to get wealth. Remembering this is an important statement: "People value you based on your ability to solve problems." The reason why you pay a doctor, a lawyer, or a mechanic is because of what they know that you do not. What they know about their area of expertise is why we pay them for what they do.

God knows every need on the earth and what it would take to resolve them. We are only one wisdom idea away from changing the world. God giving you one idea on how to solve a problem on earth is the only thing separating you from where you are to a greater place of wealth and influence. God has a solution for every problem on earth. We just need His wisdom as to how to solve it.

There was a man named George Washington Carver that asked God to show him everything there was to know about the peanut. As you may know, God revealed to him over 300 products from peanuts alone. So, if God can do that for him with a peanut, what else can God do? When we get to heaven, I wonder how many other things God could have used that no one ever tapped into.

In 2008, Elon Musk and Tesla started releasing their first electric cars to be bought and sold on the car market. There were other electric cars before, but Tesla was the first to be seen and respected as an electric car manufacturer.

That idea was out there, just waiting for someone with wisdom to make it happen on Earth. God knows what is needed out there. You just need the wisdom to solve it.

How do you know that when you sow this time, God will not give you an idea that could generate generational wealth for you? I want to encourage you not to sit on any idea God brings to you in this season. I believe we are in a season when God is raising up Josephs to be the answer for the droughts, famines, and problems that are on the earth.

God is looking for people whom He can give through, not just give to. This is the reason why He wants to know if He can trust you to sow a Wisdom Seed. If God can trust you with the seed, He knows He can trust you with the harvest. The harvest can come in many forms, just like the seed can be in many forms. God uses many forms in both. The question is, "Do you have faith to trust, believe, and obey?" For if you do, you are on the verge of the greatest breakthroughs of your life. God is ready, are you?

I want to pray for you that God will give you wisdom, ideas, and power to get wealth so that God may establish His covenant on the earth.

"Father, I pray in Jesus's name that you would open the eyes of Your people. I pray that they may be flooded with wisdom. I pray that as they step out in faith and sow according to your word that they will be blessed. I bind the spirit of fear and confusion that would try to hinder them. Father, I thank You for the supernatural provision and blessing that is coming to them as they obey Your word and directions. I pray the Spirit of Wisdom to be upon them and break them through every line of the devil's defense.

Lord, I ask that You grant supernatural ideas and creativity so they would see solutions to problems that have arisen or will arise on the earth. I pray they would not only have the wisdom of Solomon but also of Joseph. So they would have the answers, and You would get the glory out of their lives. Position them and give them confidence in the ideas that You are revealing to them now. I bind every spirit of fear and procrastination. I declare that they will work the ideas, inventions, and creativity You have put within them. I declare that all favor, promotion, and provision are theirs. Father, I ask that the spirit of wisdom, revelation, divine direction, and release would be upon them. I declare that they are blessed to be a blessing and that all nations of the earth would be blessed through them. In Jesus's name, Amen!"

After Solomon sowed the Wisdom Seed, God came and asked Solomon, "What do you want?" When God asks you a question like this, it is the result of favor. God gave him favor with Himself and favor with man. All because of the Wisdom Seed. He also did not waste it on things that would not generate life, finances, or victory. He asked God for Wisdom, and as a result, he obtained favor.

Why is favor important? Favor opens doors for you that money cannot. Favor keeps people up at night trying to figure out how they can bless you. Favor is when God paints a target on you that people cannot rest until they bless you.

Favor causes your enemies to have to bless you. Do not ask for wealth, do not ask for long life or even victory over your enemies, ask God for wisdom! For if you get wisdom, you will get favor. With wisdom and favor, all these other things will be added unto you. You will know how to get wealth, have a long life, and have victory over your enemies because you have wisdom and favor.

There was a person who decided they would sow a Wisdom Seed of a thousand dollars, and when they did, they received their dream job. They were relocated and had the opportunity of a lifetime. Their annual salary went up tremendously. In fact, it doubled! They did not even have to look hard to find the job. The job found them.

So, you see that favor, promotion, and provision all go hand in hand. This is what happens when a blessing comes into your life. The blessing of the Wisdom Seed is more than you can imagine.

I have heard it said, "You can have what I have when you have paid the price that I have paid." This is such a true statement. And this is what God gives you when you sow at this level. The wisdom that Solomon had comes into your world because you did what Solomon did. He is the only person in scripture that did something at the Thousand-Dollar level, and when he did, he was never the same. If God is not a respecter of persons, He will do the same thing for you.

When you are obedient and sow at this level, provision will come to you. And it may come in many different forms. One of which may be the arena of a promotion. When God wants to promote you, He often uses the Wisdom Seed to release that to you.

Remember, God uses many unique ways to bring the blessing into your life. Think of the story when the servant lost the ax head that was borrowed. Elisha told the man to throw a branch into the river, and it caused the ax head to float. If God can use a branch, God can use a Wisdom Seed.

Because of wisdom, Solomon wrote the Books of Wisdom and was the richest man ever. Even the Queen of Sheba fainted because of how wealthy he was and the glory in his life. Now, this was not a woman that was not familiar with wealth or someone that was star-struck. She had her own bag, as they would say today. So, one can only imagine what type of prestige, wealth, and excellence Solomon must have walked in.

I believe that whenever you need wisdom, pray about sowing a Wisdom Seed to activate the spirit of wisdom.

People often sow for what they want instead of what they need. What do I mean by that? They sow for wealth, health, etc. Not that this is all bad, but I believe that when you sow a Wisdom Seed, the spirit of wisdom will be released to you to give you the mind of Christ, which releases the treasures of darkness and hidden riches in secret places that have been prepared for you.

Ten

Sowing Your Wisdom Seed

After reading this book, I hope you will begin praying about sowing a Wisdom Seed. Some of you may have already sown this seed, and this book confirms what has happened to you at the Thousand-Dollar level.

I believe it is very important that whenever you sow, you know for sure that God is calling you to do so. Never sow out of compulsion or fear. Sow out of faith!

If God is calling you to sow, your spirit should have a witness that God is leading you to do so. When God is leading me to sow a large seed, my Spirit is so excited, but my mind is telling me it is crazy. However, I have noticed that even when my mind is saying, "It's crazy," my spirit is louder than my mind's rationale. I know in my knower that God is going to bless. And after I sow, I begin to expect God to move and bless. I start looking for things to begin to happen.

If you are married, pray about your seed together. I have learned that when I am sowing, I always consult with my wife. Many times, you may have a piece of the revelation, but God will reserve the rest for your spouse. I believe God does this to make each other necessary within the confines of a marriage. It helps us to become interdependent upon one another.

I encourage you never to make any major decisions without the agreement of your spouse whenever possible. I understand that all marriages are not created equal, and you should consult with your pastor if you are unsure as to how to proceed.

However, talk and pray it over with your spouse whenever you can, and give them time to hear from God for themselves. And then come back and talk about it with one another. Remember, just because you have heard from God does not mean they have and do not need to process it as well.

They will need to get confirmation for themselves. If they have questions, do not take them personally. I have learned that many times if I need to wait, God is working something out in the details of the waiting. After you get your answer (whether single or married), begin to prepare to sow and expect a harvest.

After you sow, I want to encourage you to remember the promises of the Wisdom Seed and to begin to look for God to respond to your obedience. Start looking for and expecting your harvest; do not give up on the seed until your harvest manifests.

You may want to write down what you are believing for and mark out 3-6 months after you sow and begin to look for God's wisdom, revelation, and favor in your life. Do not ever sow a seed and just leave it. A farmer sows corn and then begins to prepare for the harvest.

For the farmer, his whole job is simply to cultivate the harvest. As you sow, watch what God begins to do in your life. I am always excited after I sow, and even when the going gets rough, I remind myself and God that I have a seed in the ground. I know that I have a harvest that is coming.

No matter what happens, never give up on your harvest. Some seeds happen very fast, and some take time. However, never give up on the seed because the longer it takes, the more your blessing is accruing interest. Remember, God only delays when the blessing is accruing interest. No matter how long the wait, understand that God will make it up to you. Whether it is your preparation time, and you are wondering why it is taking so long for a promise or calling to manifest, or if it is a seed you have sown, God will make it up to you.

Eleven

Jesus Christ:
The Greatest Wisdom Seed

The greatest seed ever sown was Jesus, and God is still reaping sons and daughters today, and we are reaping from it as well. Dominion, authority, power, victory, deliverance, healing, breakthrough, and one day heaven will be ours because God sowed the Great Wisdom Seed. If you do not know Jesus, He is the greatest and wisest seed ever sown. God, our Father, sowed Him for you and me.

Philippians 2 says that "Jesus has now been given a name above any other name that at that name every knee will bow, and every tongue will confess that He is Lord." Jesus sowed His life as a seed, and God has now given it back to Him greater than ever. That is exactly what the Father does. He asks us for a seed, and then He resurrects it and gives it back greater than it has ever been before.

Jesus now has all power and authority that He makes available to His children. All we must do is receive His free gift, and we shall have eternal life. Jesus said in John 12:24, "Except a grain of wheat falls into the ground and dies it abides alone; but if it dies, it produces much fruit." Jesus died for you and me, sowed Himself into the earth, resurrected with all power in His hands, and made it available for you and me.

Just as we have been talking about sowing a financial gift, it comes back with a great blessing. Jesus sowed His life for you and me so we can have abundant life. He did not die just to save us from hell. He died to give us abundant life now. He sowed His life so He could give us a greater and more abundant life back.

Now because of that, He is reaping millions of sons and daughters. *Would you like to be one today?*

If so, just pray this prayer. "Lord Jesus, I come to you today, a sinner in need of a Savior. I believe you came, you died, you were buried, and rose again on the third day that I might have abundant life. Thank you for sowing Your life by dying for me so I can have eternal life. From this day forward, I will not live for myself but for Your honor and glory. My life is forever yours, and you are forever mine. May I now sow my life as a seed for You that You may resurrect it and do more with my little than I ever could imagine. You are now my Savior, and I make you Lord by obeying and following your Word and command. In Jesus's name, Amen!"

If you prayed that prayer, your life is no longer your own. It is time for you to live for Christ and give your all to Him. Find a good gospel-preaching, soul-winning church that preaches the whole gospel. That means even the stuff people do not want to hear. Remember, if you are not challenged, you will not be changed.

You can visit our ministry at any time if you are anywhere in the Pittsburgh, PA, area.

Our web page is www.anotherlevel.church, or you can email us at info@anotherlevel.church. Leave us an email or contact us to let us know you have received Jesus in your heart.

Final Thoughts

I want to hear from you!

The Bible says that we will overcome by the blood of the Lamb and the word of our testimony. There is nothing more powerful than the power of someone's testimony. In the advertising world, they call this word of mouth. I have heard it said like this, "A person with an experience is never at mercy to a person with an argument."

I really want to hear from you. If you decide to follow the Holy Spirit and sow a Wisdom Seed, please let me know how God has moved in your life. Remember, your breakthrough is not just for you but is also for those who need their faith elevated. I believe there are going to be thousands of people that are going to experience the blessing of God because of this revelation.

As God moves in your life, please contact me at info@ anotherlevel.church and tell me about your breakthrough. I look forward to hearing how God has moved in your life. I am truly praying for you and believing for supernatural breakthroughs in every area of your life.

Thank you in advance for following the Holy Spirit, and I look forward to praising God for the breakthroughs, blessings, and praise reports that will be shared all around the world.

Jesus is the Great Wisdom Seed. Stay with Him, and you will never regret it. I am praying for you, and remember, your best and most blessed days are still in front of you! Go get 'em!

Made in the USA
Middletown, DE
04 November 2023

41937840R10060